MY **MR. GRUMPY** COLOURING BOOK

By Roger Hargreaves AND _____

It was a lovely summer evening.

Mr Grumpy was at home.

Crosspatch Cottage!

He sat down in an armchair, and picked up a book.

And then, do you know what he did?

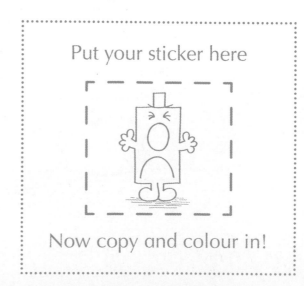

He tore all the pages out of it!

Every one!

Mr Grumpy can't stand books.

He has a shocking bad temper.

In fact, he's quite the most bad-tempered person
you can imagine.

Grumpy by name, and even more grumpy by nature!

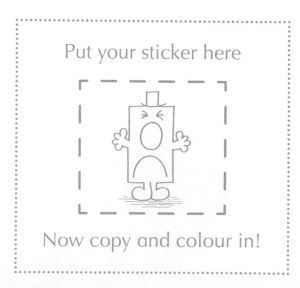

Put your sticker here

Now copy and colour in!

The following morning, he was out in his garden pulling up flowers (he couldn't stand pretty flowers growing in the garden), when out of the corner of his eye he saw a figure.

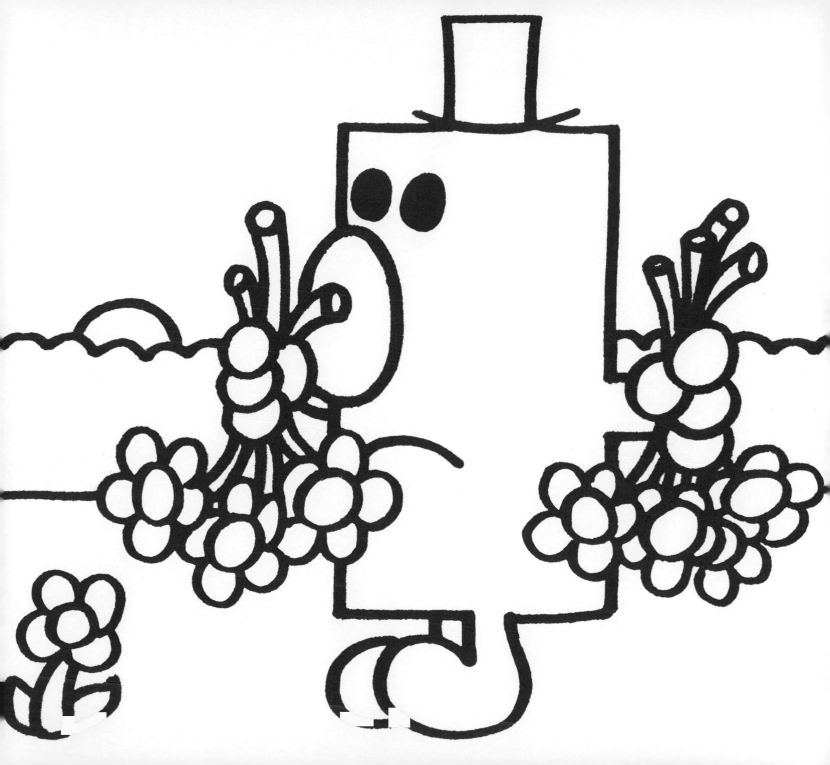

It was Mr Happy.

"Good morning," said Mr Happy.

"Good?" said Mr Grumpy. "What's good about it?"

"But …" said Mr Happy.

"But nothing," went on Mr Grumpy. "Get out of my garden!"

"I beg your pardon?" said Mr Happy.

"You heard me," snapped Mr Grumpy. "Go away!"

"I say," laughed Mr Happy. "You are a bad-tempered fellow!"

"Hmph!" grunted Mr Grumpy.

"And," went on Mr Happy, "bad-tempered fellows need to change their ways."

Put your sticker here

Now copy and colour in!

"Rubbish!" retorted Mr Grumpy, and went into his cottage, deliberately stepping on Mr Happy's foot as he passed him.

"Ouch!" said Mr Happy.

BANG! went the door of Crosspatch Cottage as Mr Grumpy slammed it behind him.

Mr Happy stood there, looking not quite as happy as he normally does.

His foot hurt!

He thought.

And thought.

And thought some more.

Then, he had an idea.

He smiled, and went to see Mr Tickle.

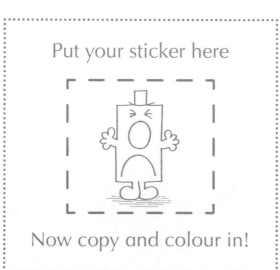

Mr Happy told Mr Tickle of his idea of how to get
Mr Grumpy to change his ways, and Mr Tickle grinned
the sort of grin that goes from ear to ear.

That is, if you have ears, which he doesn't.

"Oh," he grinned, rubbing the hands at the end of those
extraordinarily long arms of his together.
"That sounds fun!"

That afternoon, Mr Grumpy went to town, shopping.

He walked into Mr Meat's shop.

Mr Meat was a butcher.

"Give me some sausages," snapped Mr Grumpy.
"And be quick about it!"

Poor Mr Meat, who was frightened of Mr Grumpy,
did as he was told.

But, as he was doing as he was told, something
appeared through his shop doorway.

Do you know what it was?

It was an extraordinarily long arm belonging to …

Well, you can guess who it belonged to.

Can't you?

That extraordinarily long arm of Mr Tickle's came in through the door, and across the shop, and up to Mr Grumpy, and tickled him.

"Oh!" squeaked Mr Grumpy in alarm, dropping his sausages, and looking round to see what had happened.

But, could he see anything?

He could not!

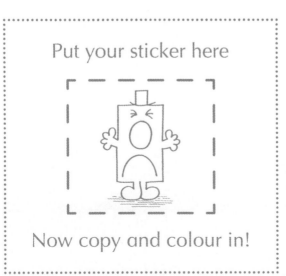

Put your sticker here

Now copy and colour in!

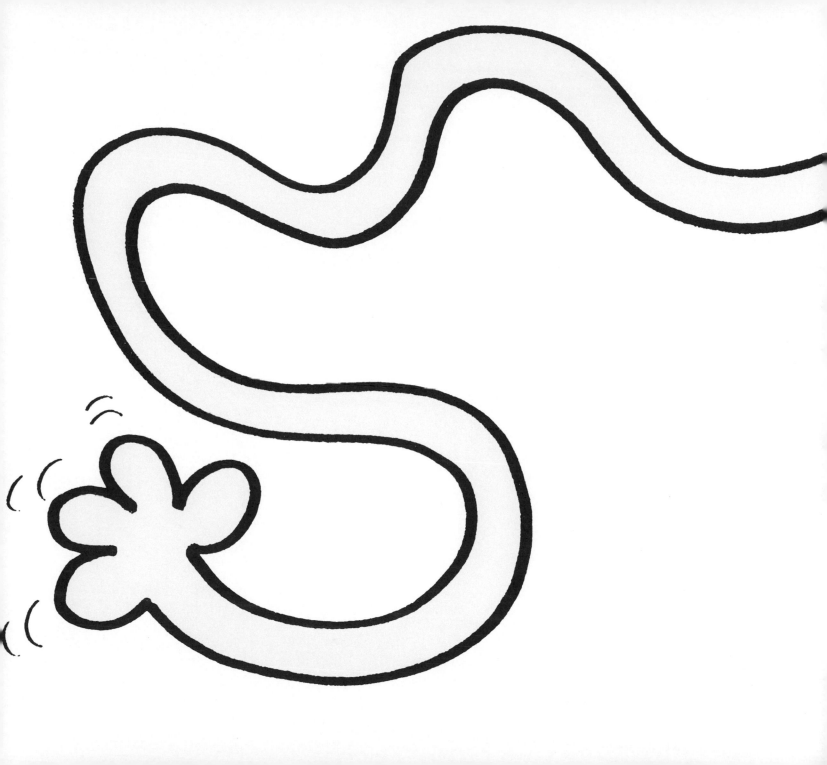

"Hmph!" grunted Mr Grumpy, and picked up his sausages, and went next door.

To the cake shop.

CRASH! went the door of the shop.

"Give me a cake," snapped Mr Grumpy. "And hurry up!"

Poor Mrs Fairy, who sold cakes, was frightened of Mr Grumpy, so did as she was told.

But, as she was doing as she was told, guess what happened?

"Oh!" squeaked Mr Grumpy, dropping his cake, and his sausages.

He just could not understand what was happening.

Put your sticker here

Now copy and colour in!

And, the same thing happened at Mr Daily's (the newspaper shop), and at Mrs Humbug's (the sweetshop), and at Mr Bottle's dairy, and at Mr Packet's (the grocer's).

It went on all afternoon!

And all afternoon, Mr Grumpy kept being tickled, and dropping his shopping, and picking it up, and being tickled, and dropping his shopping, and picking it up, and being tickled, and dropping his shopping, and …

He just could not understand it.

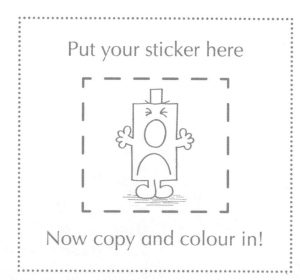

Put your sticker here

Now copy and colour in!

On his way home to Crosspatch Cottage, he met Mr Happy again.

"Hello," grinned Mr Happy. "Having a nice day?"

"Get out of my way," snapped Mr Grumpy, "before I kick you!"

But, almost before the words had passed his lips, that extraordinarily long arm of Mr Tickle's had appeared from behind a tree and tickled him yet again.

He jumped in the air, and dropped all his shopping (yet again), and fell over.

Mr Happy looked at Mr Grumpy lying amid a jumble of sausages and cake and newspapers and sweets and milk and cornflakes.

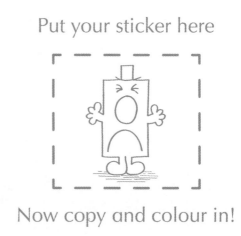

Put your sticker here

Now copy and colour in!

"I think," he laughed, "that if you were to change your ways and be not quite so bad-tempered quite so often, this sort of thing might not happen to you quite so often."

"Hmph!" grunted Mr Grumpy.

He picked up all his shopping (yet again) and went home to Crosspatch Cottage.

But on his way, he did think about what Mr Happy had said, because he very definitely did not like what had happened to him that afternoon.

Mr Happy and Mr Tickle laughed and shook hands.

Put your sticker here

Now copy and colour in!

And so, after that, Mr Grumpy did try to be not quite so bad-tempered quite so often.

And the more he tried, the less he found he was tickled, and so he tried more and more, and these days he's quite a changed person.

Why, only the other evening, he picked up a book, and do you know what?

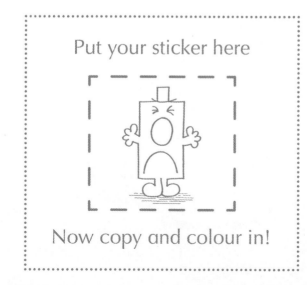

Put your sticker here

Now copy and colour in!

He only tore out one page!

I finished this book on _____ .

I am _____ years old.